I0804427

Wise Words of STEAM

100 ART WORDS EXPLAINED

JON RICHARDS

Cavendish Square

Published in 2025 by Cavendish Square Publishing, LLC
2544 Clinton Street, Buffalo, NY 14224

First published in Great Britain in 2021 by Wayland
Copyright © Hodder and Stoughton, 2021

No part of this publication may be reproduced, stored in a retrieval system, or transmitted in any form or by any means—electronic, mechanical, photocopying, recording, or otherwise—without the prior permission of the copyright owner. Request for permission should be addressed to Permissions, Cavendish Square Publishing, 2544 Clinton Street, Buffalo, NY 14224. Tel (877) 980-4450; fax (877) 980-4454.

Website: cavendishsq.com

This publication represents the opinions and views of the author based on his or her personal experience, knowledge, and research. The information in this book serves as a general guide only. The author and publisher have used their best efforts in preparing this book and disclaim liability rising directly or indirectly from the use and application of this book.

All websites were available and accurate when this book was sent to press.

Series editor: John Hort
Designed and edited by Tall Tree Ltd

Picture Credits
FC-front cover, BC-back cover, t-top, b-bottom, l-left, r-right, c-center
1–48 Sandra_M/Shutterstock.com, 4c, 14–15, 16, 17, 38t, 38b, 39t, 41t, 41b, 42c, Everett Collection/Shutterstock.com, 5t buteo/Shutterstock.com, 5b wattana/Shutterstock.com, 6–7 Krieng Meemano/Shutterstock.com, 6b Art_Textures/Shutterstock.com, 8tr UgnePouwell/Shutterstock.com, 8b Bokeh Art Photo/Shutterstock.com, 9t Luisa Puccini/Shutterstock.com, 9b aslysun/Shutterstock.com, 10c Photo_Traveller/Shutterstock.com, 11 PhotoFires/Shutterstock.com, 12tr kasha_malasha/Shutterstock.com, 12r mdlne/Shutterstock.com, 12b fatbob/Shutterstock.com, 13t Valery Rybakow/Shutterstock.com, 16t design36/Shutterstock.com, 18t Linda Macpherson/Shutterstock.com, 18b, 36tr Africa Studio/Shutterstock.com, 19t Kostikova Natalia/Shutterstock.com, 19l Heavypong/Shutterstock.com, 19b vvoe/Shutterstock.com, 20t aurelie le moigne/Shutterstock.com, 20b Mona Makela/Shutterstock.com, 21t Yulia Lyanpina/Shutterstock.com, 21c PENpics Studio/Shutterstock.com, 21b Photoillustrator/Shutterstock.com, 21bl ronstik/Shutterstock.com, 22t Helen Hotson/Shutterstock.com, 22tr Julian Rovagnati/Shutterstock.com, 22b MoinMoin/Shutterstock.com, 22cl Malysh A/Shutterstock.com, 23t Nikolayev Alexey/Shutterstock.com, 23tl Lena9208/Shutterstock.com, 23b S-BELOV/Shutterstock.com, 23bl Becky Starsmore/Shutterstock.com, 24 mv_painting/Shutterstock.com, 25 DVAO/Shutterstock.com, 25t Thomas Holt/Shutterstock.com, 25b Tattoboo/Shutterstock.com, 26b phloxii/Shutterstock.com, 27tl Johan Swanepoel/Shutterstock.com, 27tr Joseph Nicéphore Niépce/College of Liberal Arts Office of Information Technology, University of Minnesota, 27b Gruzdeva Taisiia/Shutterstock.com, 28t Trinet Uzin/Shutterstock.com, 28b Katsushika Hokusai/Metropolitan Museum of Art, 29t Nila Newsom/Shutterstock.com, 29cl Marzolino/Shutterstock.com, 29b Morphart Creation/Shutterstock.com, 30tl Master1305/Shutterstock.com, 30tr EQRoy/Shutterstock.com, 30b Toniflap/Shutterstock.com, 31t AdaCo/Shutterstock.com, 31b Gorodenkoff/Shutterstock.com, 32tr Tatjana Kruusma/Shutterstock.com, 32cl Stanislav Samoylik/Shutterstock.com, 32b Aleksandr Bel/Shutterstock.com, 33 Alhim/Shutterstock.com, 34l courtesy The Solomon R. Guggenheim Foundation Peggy Guggenheim Collection, 34br Kunal Mahto/Shutterstock.com, 35t Zerbor/Shutterstock.com, 35b TRIPLE_S/Shutterstock.com, 36 KJ Lam/Shutterstock.com, 37t Daimond Shutter/Shutterstock.com, 37c jorisvo/Shutterstock.com, 39b Robert Delauney/Musée d'Art Moderne de la Ville de Paris, 40 Eugène Delacroix/Art Institute of Chicago, 41br Alphonse Mucha/Public Domain, 42b Elena Akkurt/Shutterstock.com, 43 Weirner Pursell/United States Library of Congress's Prints and Photographs division, 44 Anton_Ivanov/Shutterstock.com, 45t Ekaterina Shagaeva/Shutterstock.com, 45b Gandolfo Cannatella/Shutterstock.com, 46b Pierre Jean Durieu/Shutterstock.com, 47cr Hillol Choudhury/Shutterstock.com, 47br Vector FX/Shutterstock.com.

Every attempt has been made to clear copyright. Should there be any inadvertent omission, please apply to the publisher for rectification.

Cataloging-in-Publication Data

Names: Richards, Jon.
Title: 100 art words explained / Jon Richards.
Description: Buffalo, New York : Cavendish Square Publishing, 2025. | Series: Wise words of STEAM | Includes index.
Identifiers: ISBN 9781502671578 (pbk.) | ISBN 9781502671585 (library bound) | ISBN 9781502671592 (ebook)
Subjects: LCSH: Art--Terminology--Juvenile literature.
Classification: LCC N34.R53 2025 | DDC 428.1--dc23

CPSIA compliance information: Batch #CSCSQ25: For further information contact Cavendish Square Publishing LLC at 1-877-980-4450.

Printed in the United States of America

Find us on

CONTENTS

AMAZING ART

For thousands of years, humans have tried to record and interpret the world around them through art, whether that takes the form of a picture on a wall or a towering statue.

1: Subject

The idea, object, or person that is being shown in the work of art.

2: Composition

The position of the subjects within the artwork.

3: Shape

The two-dimensional area covered in a work of art. A shape can be shown using an outline or by using different colors and tones.

4: Color

A color is a result of the type of light that is reflected by something back into the viewer's eye.

FANTASTIC FACT

Some of the oldest art ever discovered can be found on the island of Sulawesi, Indonesia. These cave paintings show human hands and animals, and date back nearly 35,500 years.

5: Tone

How light or dark a color appears to be. A single color can have a huge range of different tones.

6: Texture

How the surface of a work of art appears to a viewer. You can have the illusion of texture and real, tangible texture.

COLOR

A rainbow shows the whole range of colors that are visible to the naked eye. This range of colors is called the visible spectrum.

7: *Spectrum*

The full range of colors.

8: *Color wheel*

An arrangement of colors organized in a wheel, or circle. A color wheel shows the relationship between different types of color.

9: Complementary colors

Also known as opposite or contrasting colors, these are pairs of colors which – when mixed together – create tertiary colors. They are shown opposite each other on a color wheel.

10: Primary colors

These are the colors which, when mixed together, can create any other color. The three primary colors of red, blue, and yellow cannot be made by any other colors.

MEMORY GAME

There are a number of phrases, or mnemonics, you can use to remember the order of the colors of the rainbow. The correct order of colors is:

Red, Orange, Yellow, Green, Blue, Indigo, Violet

Common mnemonics include:

Read Out Your Good Book In Verse

and

Richard Of York Gave Battle In Vain

MORE COLOR

As well as the spectrum, colors come in a whole host of different tints and strengths. Artists explore and experiment with this enormous range of colors to pick exactly the right ones for their artwork.

11: *Pigment*

A substance that produces a particular color.

12: *Palette*

The range of colors used in a work of art. The word palette also refers to a flat board on which an artist mixes paints to produce new colors and tints.

13: *Fade*

When a color gradually becomes fainter.

14: *Tint*

The shade of a color.

15: *Monochrome*

When an image uses different tones from just one color.

LIGHT AND SHADE

How an artist chooses to use light and shade in an artwork can greatly affect the impact it has on a viewer, whether it's bright highlights to draw attention or dark, looming shadows to produce a feeling of uneasiness.

16: *Contrast*

When two objects or colors are very different from each other.

17: *Brightness*

The amount of light in an image or artwork.

18: *Shade/Shadow*

An area that is darker than other parts because it is sheltered from a light source.

FANTASTIC FACT

Chiaroscuro (kee-ar-os-koor-oh) is a type of art that uses strong contrast between light and dark to make the subject appear more solid. Well-known painters who used this technique include Caravaggio and Rembrandt.

19: *Highlight*

A bright or reflective part of an artwork.

MAKING A MARK

Even the greatest work of art starts off with a simple mark. Artists need to know what sort of mark would best suit the artwork they want to create.

20: ***Line***

A long, thin mark or band.

21: ***Stippling***

Creating an artwork using lots of small dots.

22: ***Crosshatching***

To create a shaded area using a group of crossing lines.

23: *Impasto*

Creating an artwork using thick layers of paint that stick out from the surface.

24: *Sketch*

A quick or unfinished drawing that is usually made with a pencil.

FANTASTIC FACT

Many artists use sketches as studies or to practice for larger artworks. Leonardo da Vinci produced thousands of different sketches on a wide range of subjects, from armored cars and flying machines to horses and human body parts.

PERSPECTIVE

Some two-dimensional artworks appear to be three-dimensional because they use perspective, giving the pictures a sense of depth and distance.

25: *Horizon*

The line where the sky appears to meet the surface.

26: *Perspective*

To give the impression of a three-dimensional view or object on a flat surface. Perspective works on the principle that objects placed farther from the viewer appear to be smaller than objects that are close to the viewer.

27: Distance

The part of a scene that is farthest from the viewer.

28: Vanishing point

The point in the distance where parallel lines appear to join up and objects appear to disappear.

MEMORY GAME

Read these two pages carefully. Then close the book and create a simple drawing that uses all of these aspects of perspective. Can you label them as well?

29: Foreground

The part of a scene that is closest to the viewer.

SIZE AND SHAPE

Size may not be everything, but using and playing with shape, structure, and proportion can affect how works of art influence their audience.

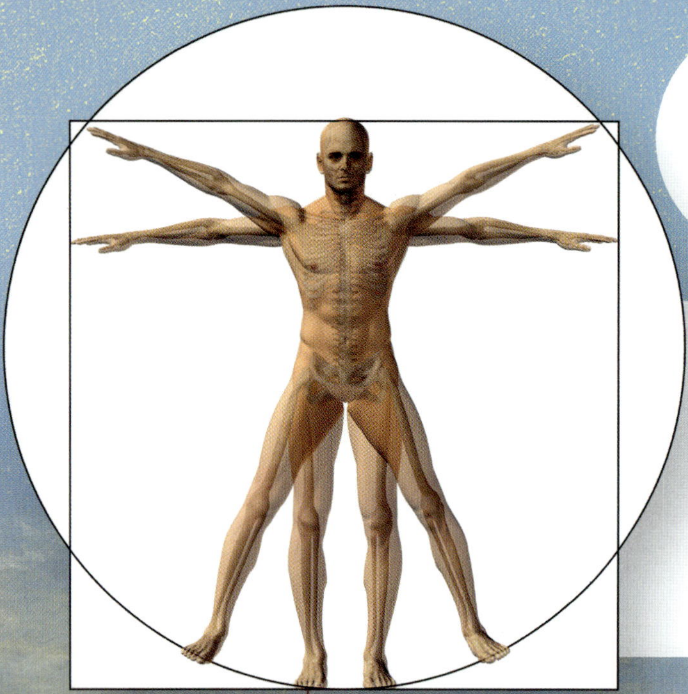

30: ***Scale***

The size of an object in relation to something else.

31: ***Proportion***

The size of part of an object when compared with the whole object. Each of the body parts in the image to the left are in proportion with the figure as a whole.

32: ***Landscape***

An image that is wider than it is tall. The word "landscape" is also used to describe an artwork that shows a natural view.

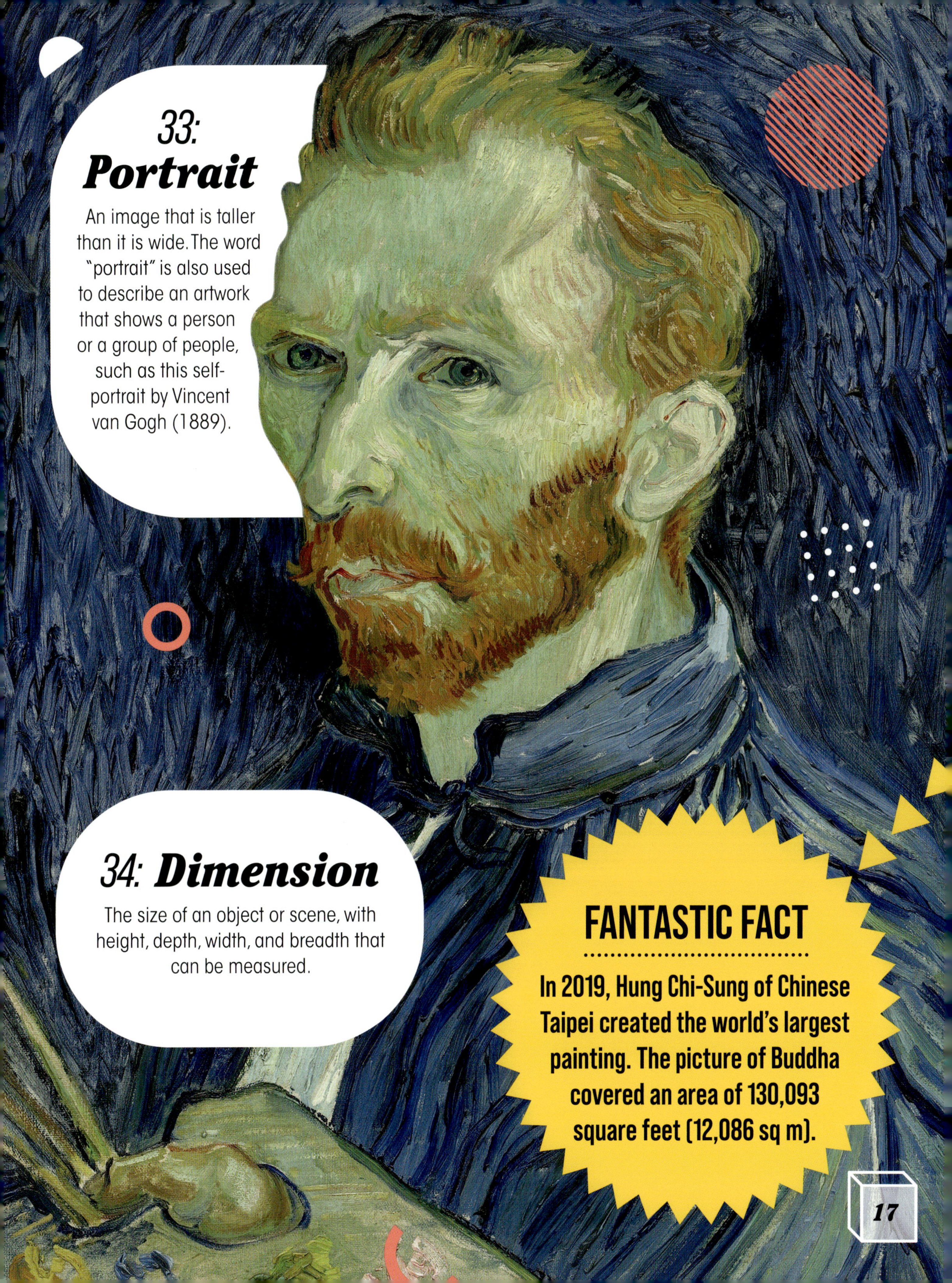

33: **Portrait**

An image that is taller than it is wide. The word "portrait" is also used to describe an artwork that shows a person or a group of people, such as this self-portrait by Vincent van Gogh (1889).

34: **Dimension**

The size of an object or scene, with height, depth, width, and breadth that can be measured.

FANTASTIC FACT

In 2019, Hung Chi-Sung of Chinese Taipei created the world's largest painting. The picture of Buddha covered an area of 130,093 square feet (12,086 sq m).

PAINTS AND MEDIA

In order to produce the effect and the style that they want to achieve, an artist has to decide on the medium before they've even put pen, pencil, or brush to paper.

35: *Medium*

The materials used to create an artwork.

36: *Charcoal*

A black form of carbon that is made by heating wood. It produces a dark gray mark.

37: **Pencil**

A writing/drawing instrument that uses a stick of graphite, called "lead," to produce a dark gray mark. Pencil lead comes in different levels of hardness to produce different shades.

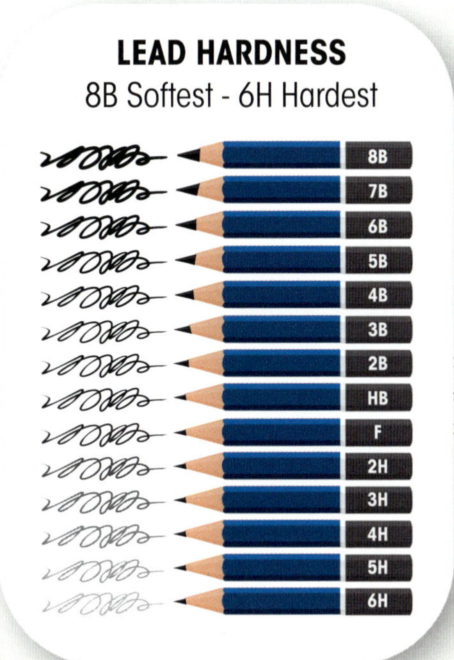

38: **Pen**

A writing/drawing instrument that uses ink to produce a mark. Pens deliver the ink using a pointed nib, a felt tip, or a rolling ball.

39: **Soft pastel**

These use a gum or clay as a binder to hold powdered pigment together, giving them a "chalky" feel.

FANTASTIC FACT

Prehistoric artists created their paints using natural materials, such as claylike ochre, which produces a range of yellows and browns, and charcoal, for grays and blacks.

40: **Oil pastel**

These use an oily binder to hold the pigment together. Oil pastels produce a harder edge than soft pastels.

41: **Ink**

A colored liquid that is used to write or draw.

42: **Watercolor**

A type of paint that uses a water-soluble binder and is made thinner by adding more water.

43: **Oil paint**

A type of paint that uses a pigment mixed with an oil that dries, such as linseed oil.

44: *Gouache*

An opaque watercolor paint.

FANTASTIC FACT

The earliest oil painting dates from the 600s CE, when the walls of a cave in Afghanistan were decorated using paints made with walnut or poppy oil.

45: *Acrylic*

A type of paint that uses a pigment mixed with an acrylic emulsion. Acrylic paints can be mixed with water when they are wet, but they are water-resistant when they have dried.

EQUIPMENT

As well as pens, pencils, and paints, an artist needs a surface to put the artwork on and tools to apply the color.

46: *Canvas*

The stretched material that an artist paints on.

47: *Easel*

A frame that holds an artwork while an artist works on it.

48: Brush

A tool that has short bristles or hairs on the end of a stick. The bristles pick up ink or paint for the artist to transfer to the artwork.

49: Palette knife

A painting knife, or palette knife, is an artist's tool that uses a long, thin blade to transfer the paint, rather than the bristles of a brush.

ART FORMS

Artists can work in a huge range of forms, from traditional drawing and painting, to mixed media that uses elements from visual and even audio sources.

50: *Painting*

An artwork made using paint.

51: *Drawing*

An artwork made using a pen, pencil, or crayon instead of paint.

52: *Photograph*

An image recorded on light-sensitive film or digitally.

FANTASTIC FACT

In 1826, French scientist Joseph Nicéphore Niépce took the world's first photograph. It shows a view from a window at his country home in France. It took several hours for the image to be recorded onto the light-sensitive film.

53: *Mixed media*

Artwork that uses several different mediums, such as paper, textiles, and wood.

54: Collage

A work of art made by sticking together scraps and pieces of different materials.

55: Printmaking

Making artworks by pushing textiles or paper onto blocks or plates that have a design etched into them and are covered with ink. *The Great Wave of Kangawa* by Hokusai (left) is a Japanese woodcut print.

56: **Fresco**

An artwork that is painted onto wet plaster that is covering a wall or ceiling. The paint colors sink into the plaster and are fixed when the plaster dries.

57: **Etching**

Using an acid to cut a design into a surface. The etched surface is then covered with ink and the design printed onto paper or material.

58: **Engraving**

An artwork that involves carving a design into a surface.

59: *Montage*

Using separate images or pieces of film and merging them together to create a new artwork.

60: *Mural*

An artwork that has been created on a wall.

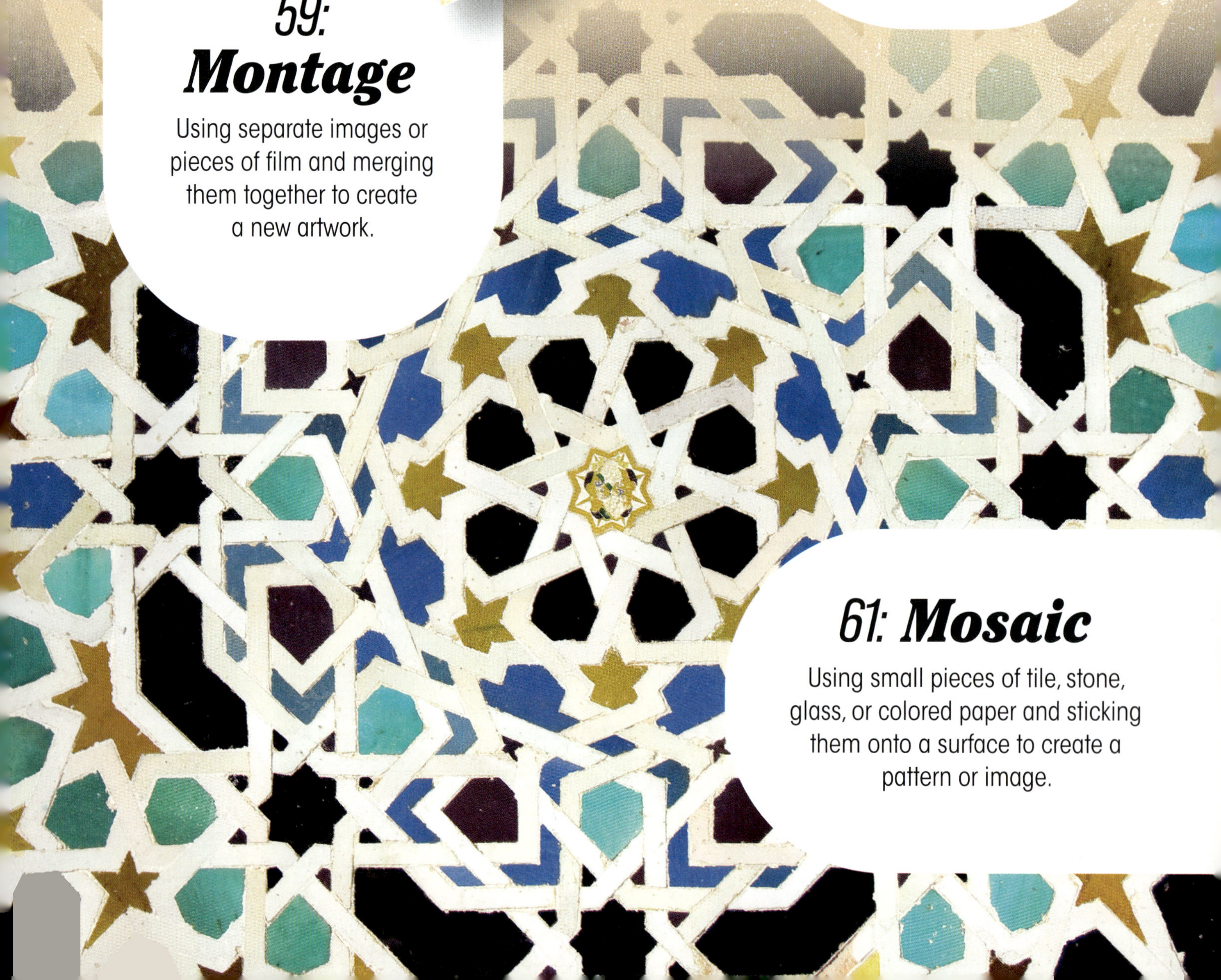

61: *Mosaic*

Using small pieces of tile, stone, glass, or colored paper and sticking them onto a surface to create a pattern or image.

62: *Multimedia*

A piece of art that combines elements from different media sources, such as sounds and moving images.

MEMORY GAME

Read these definitions out loud to a group of friends or classmates. Then test them to see who can remember them the best.

63: *New media*

Using the latest digital technology to create an artwork.

POTTERY

Turning clay into useful and sometimes highly decorated objects is one of the oldest forms of art.

64: *Clay*

A moldable material that can be shaped when it is wet. It becomes hard when it has dried and been baked in a kiln.

65: *Pottery*

The use of clay to make bowls, dishes, cups, and pieces of art.

66: *Potter's wheel*

A spinning wheel that is used to shape clay into pots.

67: *Glaze*

A special liquid that is used to cover pottery. Once applied, it hardens to form a protective outer coating.

68: *Kiln*

A type of oven that is used to bake clay once it has been shaped.

FANTASTIC FACT

The earliest type of pottery produced is known as earthenware. Some examples are more than 20,000 years old.

SCULPTURE

Many artists chose to work in three dimensions, shaping and building artworks using clay, stone, wood, metal, and even everyday objects.

69: *Sculpture*

An artwork made by shaping materials to create a three-dimensional object. Sculptures can be produced by: carving a material, such as wood and stone; casting metal or plaster; modeling; or constructing.

70: *Statue*

A large sculpture that usually shows a person or an animal.

71: Chisel

A tool with a long blade that is used to carve stone, wood, or metal.

72: Mallet

A type of hammer that has a large wooden or rubber head. Sculptors use a mallet to hit a chisel.

73: Cast

Create an object by pouring liquid metal or plaster into a mold and leaving it to harden.

TEXTILES

As well as making the clothes you wear every day, textiles can be used to produce amazing artworks, including ornate carpets, wall hangings, and even three-dimensional sculptures.

74: Cloth

A piece of fabric made by weaving, knitting, or squashing fibers together. The fibers can be natural, such as wool or cotton, or they can be artificial, such as nylon.

75: Weaving

Interlacing threads together to produce cloth.

76: Loom

A machine used to weave threads together to produce cloth.

77: Tapestry

An image made by weaving colored thread together or by embroidering the threads into a piece of cloth.

78: Dyeing

Changing the color of something by soaking it in a colored chemical called a dye.

FANTASTIC FACT

The Bayeux Tapestry is an embroidered cloth showing the events around the Battle of Hastings in 1066 and the rise of William the Conqueror to the English throne. It's nearly 230 feet (70 m) long and is made up of 58 scenes, showing 626 characters and 202 horses.

TYPES OF ART

Throughout the history of art, styles have changed to reflect the fashion of the day and the desire by some artists to push and even break the boundaries of traditional art. This has created an enormous range of visual styles.

79: Renaissance

"Renaissance" comes from the French for "rebirth" and it refers to a rediscovery of the art and culture of the classical worlds of ancient Greece and Rome. Renaissance artists include Leonardo da Vinci, Michelangelo, and Raphael.

80: Baroque

A style of art that was popular in Europe from the early 1600s until the mid-1700s. It features lots of detail, contrast, and rich colors. Baroque artists include Rubens, van Dyck, Rembrandt, Caravaggio, and Velázquez.

81: **Neoclassicism**

A style of art that was popular from the mid-1700s and into the 1800s. It was influenced by the classical worlds of ancient Greece and Rome and inspired by recent archaeological discoveries of Greek and Roman buildings and artifacts.

82: **Abstract**

A style of art that doesn't seem to feature anything you might see in the world around you. The term "abstract" comes from the word "abstraction," meaning to be taken from reality. Artists began using abstract styles towards the end of the 1800s.

83:
Romanticism

An art movement that was popular throughout the 1800s. The art focuses on the feelings and emotions of the artist and features heroic subjects and dramatic landscapes.

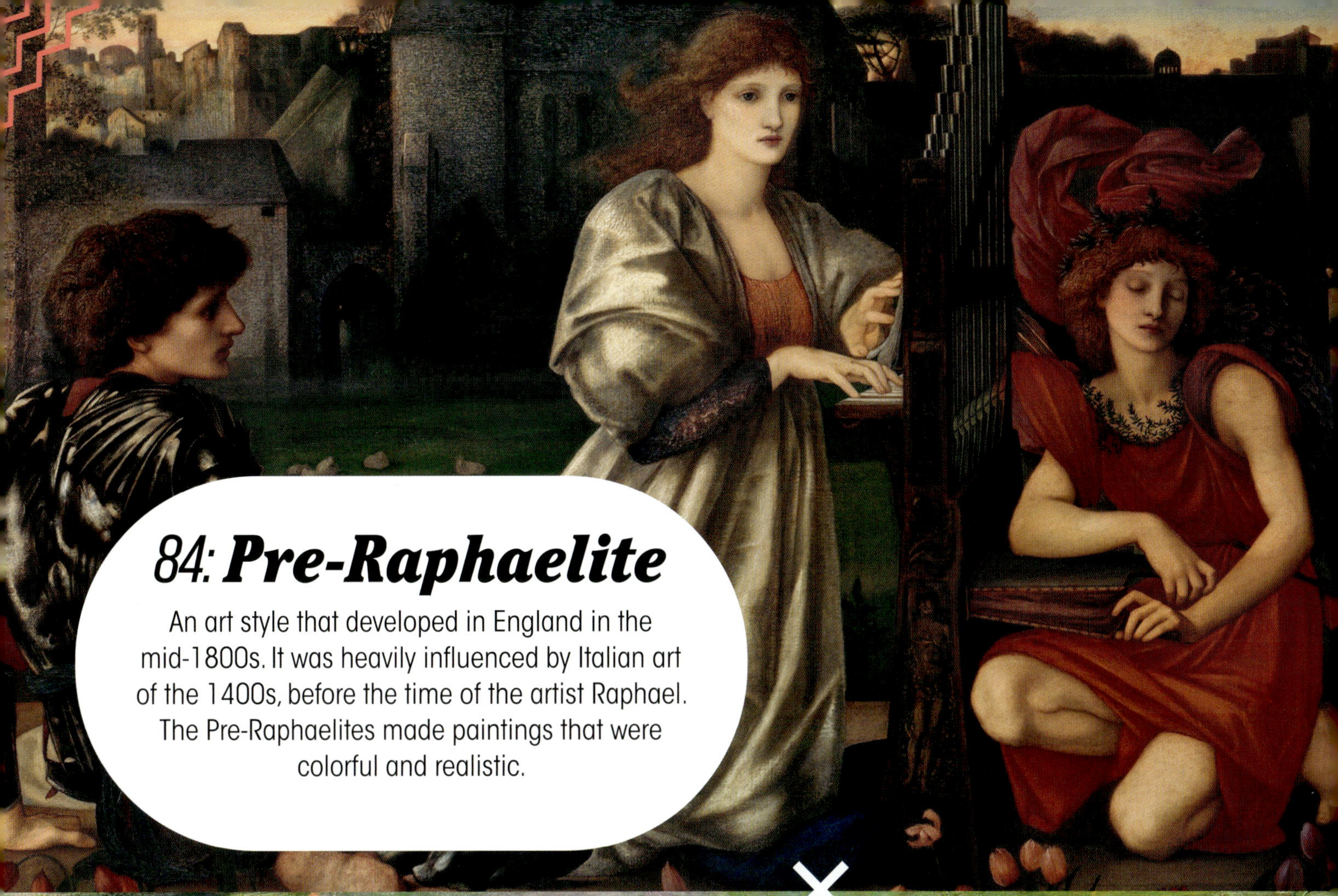

84: **Pre-Raphaelite**

An art style that developed in England in the mid-1800s. It was heavily influenced by Italian art of the 1400s, before the time of the artist Raphael. The Pre-Raphaelites made paintings that were colorful and realistic.

85: **Impressionism**

A style of art that developed in France in the 1860s and was based on painting on the spot, rather than in a studio from sketches. The art tries to capture an impression of the subject, the light and the atmosphere, rather than an accurate reflection of what's being shown.

86: **Art Nouveau**

An art style from the 1890s to the 1910s. It features lots of flowing curves and intricate designs.

87: Cubism

A style of art that developed in the early 1900s. It takes a subject and breaks it up into different parts, viewing those parts from different angles and with abstract forms.

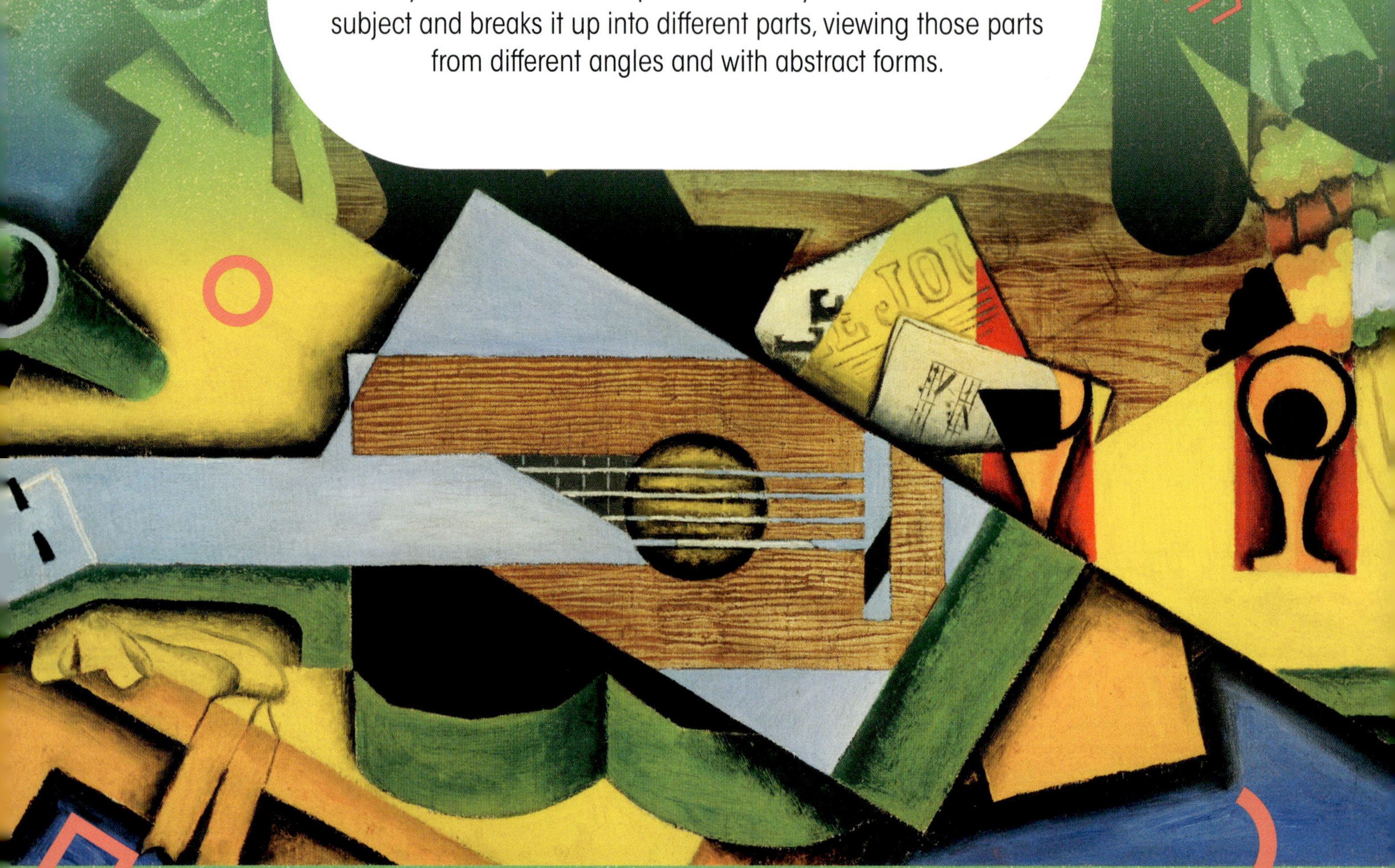

88: Surrealism

A style developed in the 1920s. Surrealist artists featured "normal" everyday objects, but showed them in unnatural, illogical, and extreme situations.

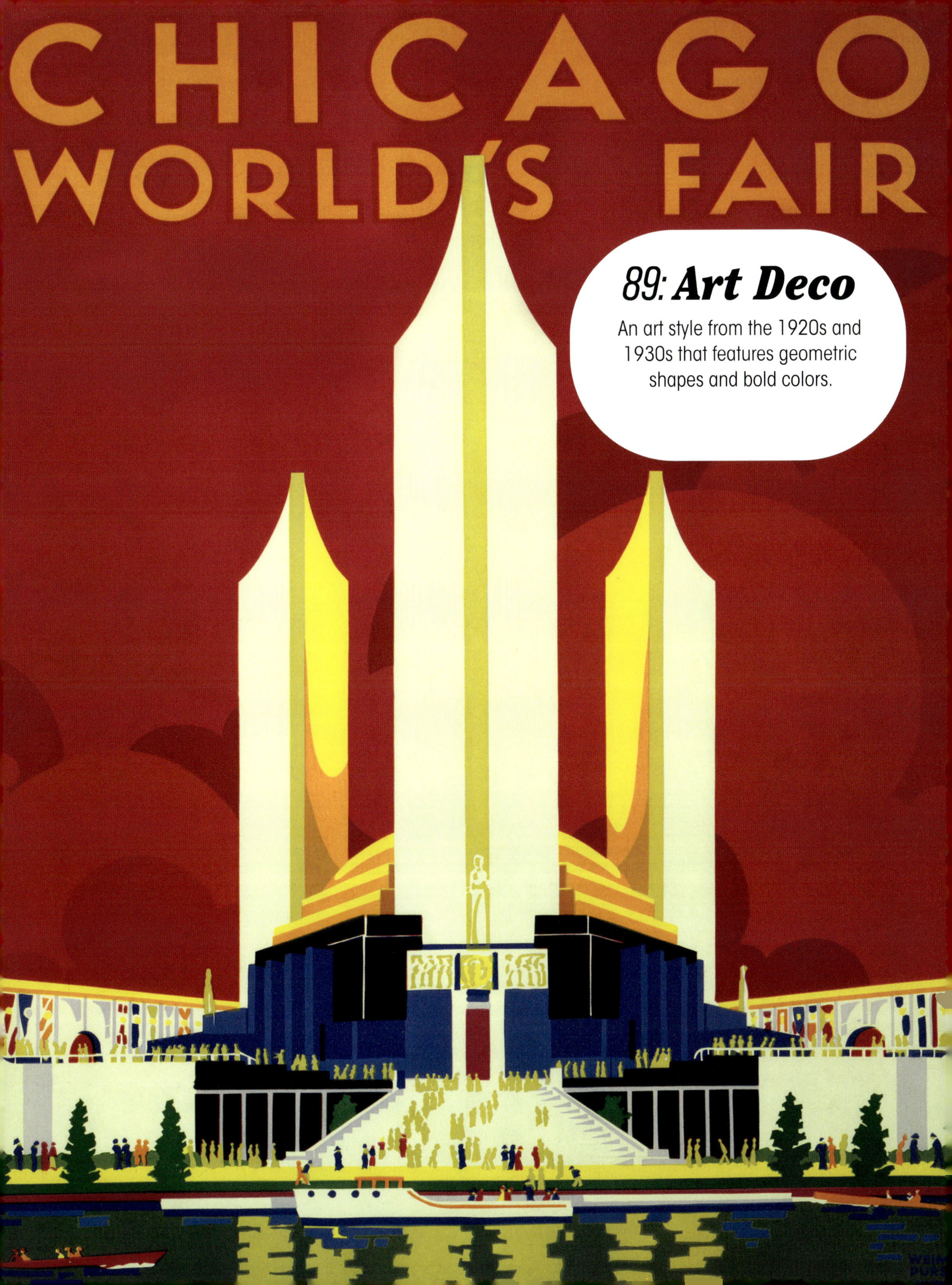

89: Art Deco

An art style from the 1920s and 1930s that features geometric shapes and bold colors.

ON DISPLAY

The walls and spaces in an art gallery are filled with works of art that can cover thousands of years of history. Alternatively, they can show the artworks of a single artist produced in a short period of time.

90: *Gallery*

A place where artworks are displayed and sold.

91: *Exhibition*

A display of artworks that is open to the public, usually in an art gallery or museum.

92: *Retrospective*

An exhibition that features the work of a single artist, looking back on the work they've completed over a period of time.

FANTASTIC FACT

The Louvre Museum in Paris, France, is the most popular art gallery in the world. Every year, more than 10 million people visit the museum to see its exhibits.

93: *Diptych*

An artwork that is made from two panels that are joined by a hinge and can be closed up like a book.

94: *Triptych*

An artwork that is made from three hinged panels.

SEEING IS BELIEVING?

Sometimes works of art are created to trick the viewer's mind into thinking they are something else.

95: *Illusion*

An image that creates a false impression. In the image below, it appears that one end of the rectangle is darker than the other, but they are in fact the same shade.

96: *Trompe-l'oeil*

A painting that is designed to make the viewer believe that something is actually there. The term "Trompe-l'oeil" comes from the French meaning "deceives the eye."

97: After image

An image that continues to appear in the eyes even when the viewer has closed them or looked away.

98: Ambiguous image

An image that could be two or more different things. The below image, for example, looks like both a vase and two faces.

99: Forced perspective

A type of optical illusion that makes something appear to be closer, farther away, bigger, or smaller than it actually is.

100: Impossible object

A drawing of an object that could not exist in three dimensions.

INDEX